WOMEN'S SOCCER

THE PASSIONATE GAME

WOMEN'S

SOCCER

BARBARA STEWART with **HELEN STOUMBOS**

Foreword by **CHARMAINE HOOPER**

Photographs by **J. BRETT** & **PAM WHITESELL**

GREYSTONE BOOKS

Douglas & McIntyre Publishing Group

Vancouver/Toronto/Berkeley

Greystone Books
A division of Douglas & McIntyre Ltd.
2323 Quebec Street, Suite 201
Vancouver, British Columbia
Canada V5T 4S7
www.greystonebooks.com

National Library of Canada Cataloguing in Publication Data
Stewart, Barbara, 1960–
    Women's soccer : the passionate game / Barbara Stewart with
    Helen Stoumbos.

    ISBN 1-55365-005-0

    1. Soccer for women. I. Stoumbos, Helen. II. Title.
GV944.5.S73 2003   796.334′082   C2003-910652-7

Library of Congress Cataloguing-in-Publication Data
Stewart, Barbara, 1960–
    Women's soccer: the passionate game / Barbara Stewart with
    Helen Stoumbos ; photographs by Brett and Pam Whitesell.
    p. cm.
    ISBN 1-55365-005-0 (cloth: alk. paper)
    1. Soccer for women. 2. Soccer for women—Pictorial works.
    I. Stoumbos, Helen. II. Title.
    GV944.5.S84 2003
    796.334′082—dc21   2003051607

Editing by Mary Schendlinger
Jacket design by Jessica Sullivan
Interior design by Peter Cocking & Bonne Zabolotney
Front jacket photograph: Kristine Lilly, number 13 (U.S.A.),
and Karina LeBlanc (Canada), Gold Cup, July 2000.
Front flap photograph: Brandi Chastain (U.S.A.) and teammates, Women's
World Cup, Pasadena, 1999.
Back jacket photographs, l to r: Linda Medalen (Norway) and Charmaine
Hooper (Canada); Silvana Burtini, number 17 (Canada); Mia Hamm (U.S.A.).
All jacket photographs by J. Brett and Pam Whitesell
Interior photos by J. Brett and Pam Whitesell, unless credited otherwise
Printed and bound in Canada by Friesens
Printed on acid-free paper
Distributed in the U.S. by Publishers Group West

We gratefully acknowledge the financial support of the Canada Council for
the Arts, the British Columbia Arts Council, and the Government of Canada
through the Book Publishing Industry Development Program (BPIDP) for
our publishing activities.

CONTENTS

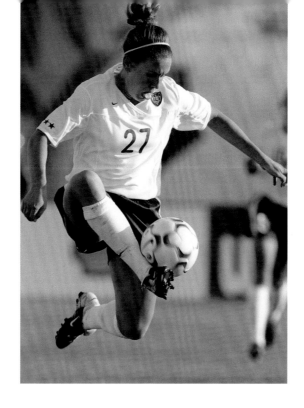

◀ Heather O'Reilly (U.S.A.)
was named to the All-
Tournament Team in
2002 when the U.S.A.
won the inaugural FIFA
Under-19 Women's World
Championship.

I   **FOREWORD: CHARMAINE HOOPER**

CHAPTER 1: TWO DAYS THAT CHANGED THE WORLD

5   *Day 1: November 30, 1991, Tianhe Stadium, Guangzhou, Southern China*
The Women's World Cup Is Born

15   *Day 2: July 10, 1999, Rose Bowl, Pasadena, California*
The Thrill of Victory

CHAPTER 2: HOW WE GOT HERE

33   The Herstory of the Game

46   Title IX and After

CHAPTER 3: WOMEN'S SOCCER AND THE OLYMPICS

49   Atlanta, 1996: Lighting the Torch

61   Sydney, 2000: The Flame Burns On

CHAPTER 4: AT THE TOP OF THEIR GAME

77   Women's Soccer Turns Pro

CHAPTER 5: IT'S A SMALL WORLD

99   The 2003 World Cup and Beyond

120   A Look Ahead

122   **ACKNOWLEDGMENTS**

◄ Charmaine Hooper, number
10 (Canada), at right, battles
Linda Medalen, also number
10 (Norway), for the ball.

FOREWORD

Charmaine Hooper

Imagine your dream job, where you get to do something you love day in, day out. People come and watch you at your job, to cheer you on and support you to keep doing your best. Welcome to my world, the world of women's soccer!

I'm truly blessed, because I get to spend my days playing the greatest sport on earth with some of the most wonderful people I've ever known. As an athlete, it's always your goal to play your sport at the highest level possible. Fortunately for me, I've gotten to live this dream both as a member of the Canada National Team and as a pro, playing with the Atlanta Beat of the Women's United Soccer Association.

Just in my lifetime, women's soccer has grown from a relatively obscure recreational diversion to the fastest growing team sport in the world. Participation has expanded from a few thousand to thirty million people around the world in less than forty years, and where once women had the challenge of fielding just half a dozen teams for an international tournament, FIFA now recognizes women's soccer teams from more than one hundred countries.

Women of my mother's generation had to content themselves with inadequately funded soccer programs at college and limited opportunities to play the game beyond university, but now women's soccer is a big part of college programs in the United States and provides a range of top-notch players to national, Olympic, and professional teams. I can't imagine a better time for soccer players.

It would be an understatement to say that soccer changed my life. Not only has it given me the opportunity to see the world and to make lasting friendships in countries I might otherwise only have dreamed about, the sport has also helped me grow as an athlete, as a coach, and, more importantly, as a person.

The Passionate Game really is the perfect title for a book like this. Women's soccer is a game that fans, players, and coaches across the world are learning to love. This book captures that passion, and brings the past, present, and future of the game to life. It's a great introduction to the sport of soccer and the personalities that make the game what it is. More than that, I hope it's a starting point for women of all ages to get involved in the game as players, coaches, referees, and fans. It's the people involved in soccer who make it the greatest sport on earth.

So enjoy *The Passionate Game*. May it encourage you to get your own kick out of women's soccer, and to gather your own memories that will last a lifetime.

1

Two Days that Changed the World

Day I: November 30, 1991
Tianhe Stadium, Guangzhou, Southern China
The Women's World Cup Is Born

The crowd was on the edge of its collective seat. A cool wind was blowing in from the north, but that didn't chill the enthusiasm of 65,000 or so soccer fans who had gathered to watch history in the making.

It was the final of the first-ever FIFA-sanctioned Women's World Cup. The players were ready—at one end of the field was the U.S.A. National Team, their white shorts and jerseys trimmed with

Linda Medalen, number 10
(Norway), fights Team U.S.A.'s
Joy Fawcett for the ball at the
Women's World Cup, Sweden,
1995. Norway took home the
gold and the Americans took
the bronze. ➤

blue and red, and at the other end, in blue and gold, were the
Norwegians, a soccer powerhouse. It was a tense match from the
start, with each team cautiously feeling the other out, looking for
weaknesses, careful not to make a costly mistake.

The Americans were the favorites, having come in first in Group
B with a record of three wins, no losses, and having outscored their
opponent 9–2. Led by a trio of potent forwards dubbed the "triple-
edged sword" by the Chinese press, the U.S. breezed through the
quarter-finals and semis, beating China 4–0, then Sweden 3–2, and
made it to the final as the only undefeated team in the tournament.

Norway had had a much harder time. Considered the top
women's team in Europe, the Norwegians suffered a stunning 4–0
loss to host China in their opening game. They went on to win the
next two games, then squeaked past Italy in the quarter-final, where
they needed extra time to score the winning goal. The team came
together in the semi-final, though, and they dismissed Sweden in a
4–1 contest. Everyone expected a tight, hard-fought final, and they
weren't disappointed.

More than twenty minutes had passed without a goal when
the American striker Michelle Akers took a crisp cross-pass and
headed it into the back of the Norwegian goal. 1–0 U.S.A. But the
Norwegians were determined to get back into the game and they
fought the Americans for every inch of turf. Eight minutes later their
hard work paid off. Norway's Linda Medalen was on the receiving
end of a little chip pass, which she headed just over the outstretched

Brandi Chastain, number 6 (U.S.A.), and Mayumi Kaji (Japan) struggle for possession of the ball at the Women's World Cup, China, 1991. Photo by Daniel Motz. ▼

Victory! Team Captain April Heinrichs (U.S.A.) holds the trophy aloft for all to see at the Women's World Cup, China, 1991. Photo by Daniel Motz. ➤

arms of the American keeper. The score was tied 1–1. The teams dug deep for the extra little bit of effort that might help them win the game.

In many ways, the game itself was a tremendous victory. The story of the World Cup had started five years earlier when Ellen Willie, a FIFA delegate from Norway, stood up at the organization's congress in Mexico City and called on members to do more to further women's soccer around the world. FIFA members overwhelmingly supported the motion. They set the stage for the first sanctioned women's tournament in 1988, in China, designed as a testing ground for a world championship. The success of that tournament on the field and at the box office convinced FIFA that world was ready for women's soccer. Three years later, FIFA assembled twelve teams in China, and the Women's World Cup was born.

The games had been a hit, capturing the hearts and imaginations of fans throughout China and around the world, and this final game had become one of the most keenly anticipated and widely covered women's sporting events ever. To sharpen the excitement, it was played the day after the sold-out third-place game, when an electrified crowd had watched the highly ranked Sweden demolish Germany 4–0 in the first game in FIFA history to be refereed by a woman, Claudia de Vasconcelos of Brazil. >

Brandi Chastain— A Star for All Seasons

Chastain has done it all. She started her international career as forward for Team U.S.A., for whom she once scored a team record 5 goals in a single match, and then switched to defense. She played every minute of her team's five games in the 1998 Olympics, and a year later her left-footed penalty kick in shootout clinched the World Cup title for the Americans. Chastain had a distinguished college career at Santa Monica, where she helped her team to four straight NCAA appearances.

Along with earning more than 140 caps for international play, Chastain was also one of the first players to join the WUSA. She's had a stellar professional career, serving time as forward, midfielder, and defender.

Chastain is shown here celebrating her gold-medal-winning goal at the Women's World Cup, Pasadena, 1999.

Intensity is the name of the
game for Brandi Chastain,
number 6 (Team U.S.A.),
and Zhang Ouying (China)
at the Women's World Cup,
Pasadena, 1999. ➤

But now, all eyes and hearts were on the outcome of this game, the contest for the championship. At halftime, Norway and the U.S.A. were still tied, and going into the second half every player on the field was focused on the job at hand. They played a technically precise game, each team advancing in its turn, only to be thwarted by solid work by the defense and phenomenal goaltending at both ends. Finally, with barely three minutes left, Michelle Akers intercepted a Norwegian pass. She tapped the ball to one side, eluding Norway's looming keeper, and punched a shot at the goal. There was silence

A Kick in the Grass

The penalty kick is one of the most exciting—and nerve-wracking—plays in soccer. Nothing can beat the drama of a lone shooter going one-to-one with a goalkeeper.

A penalty kick occurs when a defender commits a serious foul, like a trip or hand ball, in her own penalty area. The referee awards the player who is fouled a free kick from the penalty marker, twelve yards in front of the net. The shooter has one chance to put it past the goalie, who must stay on the goal line until the kicker makes contact with the ball.

Penalty kicks are an exciting part of the game. If a game is tied at the end of regulation play, the referee adds extra time to the clock for sudden death overtime play (the first team to score, wins). If the teams are still tied after extra time, they go to a shootout, with five designated shooters from each team taking five penalty shots. At the end of the shootout, the team with the most goals wins.

What happens if they're still tied after the shootout? Sudden death. The teams continue to take penalty kicks, one player from each team at a time, until a winner is decided.

Michelle Akers, number 10 (U.S.A.), outruns her opponent (Germany) to take charge of the ball at the Women's World Cup, China, 1991. Photo by Phil Stephens. ▼

Three heads are better than one as China and the U.S.A. battle it out at the Women's World Cup, China, 1991. ➤

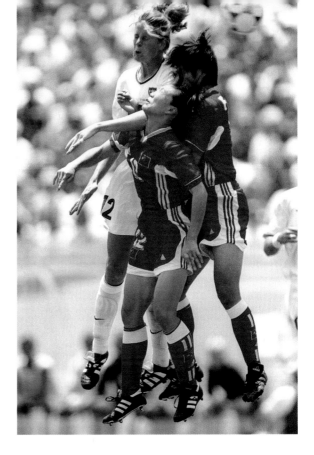

for a moment, then the American squad, and the thousands of fans who had crowded into the stadium to support them, burst into wild celebration. It was goal! America had taken on the world and won. Women's soccer would never be the same.

Day 2: July 10, 1999
Rose Bowl, Pasadena, California
The Thrill of Victory

Talk about a study in contrasts. From a cold evening in a distant city in southern China, the 1999 Women's World Cup final had moved to the media center of the universe, Los Angeles. Ninety thousand men, women, and children had packed Pasadena's Rose Bowl, along with more than two thousand media people from around the world. At home, some four million sports fans across America were glued to their TV sets. Forget about largest audience for a women's soccer game in American network history— it was the largest U.S. television audience ever, for any soccer game.

The competitors were familiar with each other and everyone who was a fan of women's soccer. At one end of the pitch was the team from China, with its speedy and aggressive forwards who had outscored their opposition 19–2 in the lead-up to the final. At the other end was Team U.S.A., a veteran-rich team that had rolled through the round robin tournament but barely made it past a

Mia Hamm – Excellence in Action

Mariel Margaret Hamm is one of the most famous and honored female soccer players in the world. In May 1999 she scored her 108th goal in international play, more than any other player, male or female. In the mid-1990s she was named U.S. Soccer's Female Athlete of the Year five years in a row, an unprecedented achievement. Her picture adorned the cover of the first-ever edition of *Sports Illustrated for Women*.

Her dominance of the sport began early. After turning heads in high school—her national team debut at age fifteen set a record—she went on to become the most impressive college women's player ever. Her University of North Carolina squad won four national championships, while Hamm was named a three-time NSCAA All-American and selected for the Soccer America's College Team of the Decade for the 1990s. Hamm ended her college career with 103 goals, 72 assists and a total of 278 points—all records likely to stand for a long time. The university retired her jersey number in 1994.

Hamm is also one of the founding members of the WUSA, and has been a powerful force in the pro league since its inception. She's also a bestselling writer, author of *Go for the Goal: A Champion's Guide to Winning in Soccer and Life.*

Homare Sawa (Japan) entered the world scene at the 1995 Women's World Cup as a teenage phenom. Not quite seventeen, she played in three of Japan's four games and turned heads with her passion and intensity. Three years later she scored an incredible 7 goals in one Asian Cup game, paving the way for Japan's trip to the 1999 World Cup. At age twenty, she was already the leading international scorer in Japanese history. Sawa is shown here in a game against Russia. ➤

surprising German squad in the semi-final. Perhaps, some commentators speculated, the Americans were too old and too slow for the feisty young Chinese players.

There was a lot on the line for the Americans. Although they were once again in the hunt for the coveted cup, the ensuing years hadn't been without disappointments. In the 1995 World Cup tournament in Sweden, the U.S. had fielded a confident veteran team. But they started slow in their first game, managing only a tie against a tough squad from China. And while they handily defeated Japan 4–0 in the quarter-final, they met their match in the semi against their old rival, Norway. The Norwegians took the lead early, in the eleventh minute, as Ann Kristen Aarones headed in a Gro Espeseth corner kick. That was it for the game. Team U.S.A. kept the pressure on their opponents for the next seventy-nine minutes, but Aarones's goal stood and the Americans had to be content with a third-place finish in the tournament. Ironically, they had to beat China in the consolation game to finish in the trophies.

The U.S.A. team redeemed themselves the following year by winning the first-ever gold medal awarded in Olympic competition for women's soccer. In front of a supportive crowd of more than 76,000 fans in Athens, Georgia, the women's team defeated none other than Team China 2–1 for the gold. Still, the World Cup loss lingered in the hearts and minds of the American players. They were determined to win international bragging rights back on their home soil. >

Gao Hong—
The Great Wall of China

Few players have dominated a position in women's soccer like Gao Hong. A mainstay of the Chinese National Team, Hong has quietly established herself as one of the greatest goalkeepers in the game.

At 5'9" she's a bit smaller than the average goalkeeper. But what she lacks in size she more than makes up for in strength, agility, and reflexes. Born in 1967, she joined her country's National Team in 1989 at the age of twenty-two, and never looked back. She led China to gold medals in the 1993, 1995, and 1997 Asian Women's Championships, and helped her team take home the silver at both the Atlanta Olympics and the 1999 Women's World Cup. One of Hong's most spectacular performances took place in the 1996 Olympic Games, when she shut out the U.S.A. in a first-round match, then blocked all but 5 goals in the five games China played.

These days Hong lends her talents to the WUSA as well, having backstopped the New York Power since 2001, and more recently she has been holding down the fort for the powerful Washington Freedom. It's not the first time she's played pro, though. Hong stood tall in the Japanese pro league from 1993 to 1997.

Sun Wen (China) tries to steal the ball from Jane Tornqvist (Sweden). ▼

Zhang Ouying, number 7 (China), concentrates on keeping the ball away from Carla Overbeck (U.S.A.) during the Women's World Cup final, Pasadena, 1999. ➤

The game began at a breathtaking pace. Both teams were relatively free of injury, and the American game plan was to use their superior conditioning to tire the Chinese squad early in the match. But the team from China was up to the test, and played a sound game in their own end despite pressure from the American forwards. Fifteen minutes into it, the game had settled down, as the two teams played cat and mouse for control of the midfield. The focus was on defense, with each team trying to shut the other down. The strategy worked almost too well—at the end of regulation time the teams were locked in a scoreless draw.

Then came extra time, although the Americans were without one of their key players. Michelle Akers, hero of the 1991 tournament, had been playing a Chinese corner kick as regulation time ran out and had crashed into her own goalie, Briana Scurry. Suffering from exhaustion, dehydration, and a concussion, Akers was carried from the field on a stretcher. In extra time, the Americans threw everything they had at the Chinese, but it was the visiting squad that got the upper hand. At 9:48 of the first sudden death overtime period, Chinese defender Fan Yunjie got her head on a perfect corner kick, pounding the ball past Scurry. The game was all but over, until Kristine Lilly, an American midfielder who was also the

Helen Stoumbos— Direct Kicks

With thirty-four international games, Stoumbos is one of the most capped players in Canadian history. A fixture in the midfield for her country from 1992 to 2000, she made history in Sweden in 1995 when she scored the first-ever goal by a Canadian at a World Cup.

Stoumbos was a key playmaker in her playing days, and since retiring from the field she has put those skills to a new use—building a career in media. She worked with *Direct Kicks: Grassroots Soccer TV* from its inception in 1998, and in 2001 started the companion program, *Direct Kicks for Chicks*. By 2003 she was widely recognized as the "voice of women's soccer in Canada," as a featured commentator for women's soccer games on Rogers Sportsnet since the 1999 Women's World Cup.

A power header from Tiffeny
Milbrett, number 16 (U.S.A.),
prevents Marie-Claude Dion
(Canada) from gaining an
edge at the Women's Gold
Cup, 2000. ➤

most experienced player in the tournament, rose up and got her head on the ball at the goal line, knocking it to safety. Thanks to Lilly's work, the game was still locked in a 0–0 tie at the end of extra time. That meant only one thing—penalty shootout.

Things proceeded quickly. The first two shooters for each team found the mark, placing perfect shots past Scurry and her Chinese counterpart, Gao Hong. Then a sudden silence shrouded the stadium as midfielder Liu Ying stepped up to the penalty marker. She carefully placed her ball, and then stepped back. As she began her approach, Briana Scurry dove to her left and managed to get her hand on Ying's shot, knocking it out of harm's way. Now it was Kristine Lilly's turn. She wasted no time stepping into the ball and blowing it past the Chinese goalie. But the next Chinese shooter hit the mark as well, and knotted the score at 3 goals apiece.

There were now three shooters left, two for the U.S. and one for China. The U.S. coach, Tony DiCicco, nodded to Mia Hamm. It was an easy choice. Hamm was the all-time scoring leader in Women's World Cup play, and one of only three people in the history of FIFA to score a hundred or more goals for her country in international tournament play. But penalty kicks were never her forte. The pressure, she admitted, got to her. Hamm put her head down and stepped into the ball. 4–3.

The Chinese weren't ready to quit, though. They made their next shot and tied the game up at 4 each. The U.S. had one shooter

Linda Medalen—
Bronze, Silver, Gold

This Norwegian defender has a trophy case full of hardware. She was a member of the 1995 World Cup gold medal team and 1991 World Cup silver medal winners, the 1996 Olympic bronze medalists, and the 1993 European Championship winners. She has also earned personal awards, including both the bronze ball and bronze shoe at the 1991 World Cup. With almost 140 international appearances for her country, Medalen helped Norway win the first unofficial women's world title in 1988. She is shown here at the Women's World Cup, Pasadena, 1999.

Brazil's Katia, number 9, prepares to unleash a shot against a player from China. ▼

The sensational Sissi of Brazil outjumps the competition at the Women's World Cup, Pasadena, 1999. ➤

left, defender Brandi Chastain. Originally Chastain was not on the list of designated penalty kickers, but DiCicco had put her back on — she was a strong kicker and she liked taking penalty shots. He gave Chastain the nod. It was quite simple. If she scored, America would win the World Cup. If she missed, the shootout would continue and China would still have a chance to take the trophy.

Chastain calmly set up her ball on the penalty marker, then stepped back. On the referee's signal, she stepped quickly into the ball. It flew past the stunned Gao Hong and into the net. In her excitement, Chastain dropped to her knees and pulled off her shirt, echoing the traditional celebration of goal at the highest level of men's soccer. On her knees, her arms raised in victory, she provided photographers with one of the most famous sports shots of the twentieth century, and a whole new generation of female soccer players with the inspiration to go on playing the game they loved.

It was 1999, and women's soccer hadn't just made its mark. It had provided one of the greatest moments in American sports history, and it would never look back.

◄ Joy Fawcett, number 14
(U.S.A.), needs all of her
tremendous speed and
strength to control the ball
against Germany at the
100th anniversary of the
German Soccer Federation
(DFB), Germany, 2000.

CHAPTER

2

How We Got Here

The Herstory of the Game

The last twenty years have seen an unprecedented rise in women's sports, particularly team sports like baseball, hockey, basketball, rugby—and, of course, soccer. It's hard to imagine how far we've come in such a short time. Not so long ago, these sorts of team sports, with their body contact and physical demands, were considered unlady-like, and not suitable for proper girls.

Well, things have changed, and women's soccer has helped lead the way.

Women have been playing soccer for centuries, if not millennia, and have played a part in the development of the sport since its very beginning. Researchers believe that various forms of soccer have been played since the dawn of human history, and thanks to two-thousand-year-old Chinese paintings that show women playing an early version of soccer, we know that the girls were alive and kicking from the start. The ancient Romans were also big soccer fans, who favored spectacular and violent games. Records tell of a match played at an early Olympic Games after which almost half of the fifty-four players on the field wound up in hospital. Roman civilization was highly segregated when it came to the sexes, so it is unlikely that any women were on that pitch, but we do know that a thousand years later females took to the fields and streets alongside their brothers, husbands, and fathers in that crazy British pastime known as mob ball. A blend of soccer, warfare, and insanity, mob ball pitted dozens of players from neighboring communities against one another. It was immensely popular for a time—so popular, in fact, that in the 1300s King Edward banned it from London's streets. He complained about the "many evils" that may arise and "great noise in the city caused by hustling over large balls," and vowed to imprison any man or woman caught playing the game.

Despite ongoing prohibitions, the sport continued to flourish in England. Still, it was not codified and it was fraught with ritualistic elements and overtones of pagan fertility rites. Some scholars see the

April Heinrichs— Leading the Way

Player, coach, and sports pioneer, April Heinrichs is one of the most significant names in the history of women's soccer. She served as captain of the 1991 U.S. Women's National Team, which won the first World Cup, and she went on to become head coach of the team.

At the University of North Carolina, Heinrichs was named First-Team All-American three times. She won U.S. Soccer Female Athlete of the Year in both 1986 and 1989, and she became the first women's soccer player in UNC history to have her jersey number retired.

After a standout international career, during which she scored 38 goals in forty-seven international games, Heinrichs moved into coaching. In 1995 she joined the U.S. National Team as an assistant, helping to take the gold at the 1996 Olympics. She then worked as head coach at universities and with the U.S. U-16 team, before taking charge of the National Team program in 2000.

April Heinrichs is the first female player to be inducted into the U.S. Soccer Hall of Fame.

soccer ball as a representative of the sun, with teams struggling to gain control over it in order to ensure a bountiful harvest. As fanciful as these ideas seem, there was certainly more afoot than a simple game. It's no coincidence that the famous late seventeenth-century women's soccer games in Inveresk, a Scottish town near Loch Ness, pitted married women against unmarried ones, all of them kicking an inflated pig's bladder through the highlands and heather. The games were as much about catching the eye of a potential husband as they were about the thrill of victory and the agony of defeat.

It was during the mid-1800s that modern soccer began to develop on the playing fields of England's public schools. At Cambridge University in 1848, representatives from all the great football playing schools got together to work out a set of standardized rules. While they could agree on rules to ban tripping, and gouging, and shin-kicking, a huge rift developed over a proposed rule prohibiting players from carrying the ball. The representatives from rugby angrily withdrew from the talks. Fifteen years later, the Football Association was formed. The organization standardized the size and weight of balls and laid out the rules of soccer, which clearly outlawed any carrying of the ball. At that point soccer and rugby went their separate ways, never to meet again.

Women were on the periphery of organized soccer from the beginning. In part it was because public schools were for men only, but as well, polite society at the time frowned on women who engaged in strenuous exercise. Doctors believed such activity could injure the reproductive system or simply make women too manly to have children. But women went on enjoying the game, and soon soccer spread to women's colleges. In 1877, Girton, the women's campus at Cambridge, built a gymnasium and encouraged women to take up sports, including soccer. Within a few years there were women's teams in clubs around Britain. Most famous of all was Dick Kerr Ladies XI. Named for its sponsor, an electrical company in Preston, and for the eleven players on the team, the club played against amateur men's teams throughout England. In the 1920s, on a tour of the United States, they racked up an impressive record of three wins, two losses, and two ties.

Meanwhile, buoyed by the growth of the game, women approached the Football Association for official status and a set of rules specifically designed for the female game. Association organizers turned down their request, saying that they didn't want to be held responsible for any injuries that might occur. It was a typical attitude for the times. As the women's suffrage and temperance movements show, women were becoming increasingly more organized and political, threatening the existing male authority.

Carolina Morace— Behind the Bench

There's one thing harder than playing soccer at an elite level, and that's coaching some of the best players in the game. Carolina Morace of Italy has done both.

In her playing days, she was the top female soccer player in Italy—perhaps even Europe. Morace was only fourteen years old when she joined Italy's National Team. She played for her country for twenty years, amassing 105 goals in 150 international games. At the same time, she led her local women's pro team to twelve league championships and scored almost 480 goals in a fifteen-year career.

After she hung up the cleats, Morace went on to provide expert commentary for Telemontecarlo, one of Italy's top TV networks, to serve briefly as head coach for Viterbese, a professional men's team (a first, not only in Italy but perhaps the world), and, in 2000, to take over as head coach of Italy's national women's team.

Undaunted by the FA's official rejection, women's soccer kept growing, particularly during and just after World War I, when male teams were decimated. Women working in factories organized teams and played matches, often to raise money for the war effort. The Dick Kerr Ladies became the standard bearer for women's soccer at this time, and a huge draw for charity matches both at home and abroad—the team almost always attracted crowds of ten thousand or more. On Boxing Day of 1920, 53,000 fans watched their match against St. Helens at Everton FC's Goodison Park.

Meanwhile, the sport was catching on in the United States as well. At any time when women's team sports such as baseball and hockey were being played across North America, women's soccer made inroads. Women were being accepted as a part of the game, and several colleges picked it up as a regular sport. In 1920 a woman named Doris Clark became manager of the McKinley Park Football Club in Sacramento. She was the first woman to hold such a position with a sanctioned team. That same year, Helen Clark (no relation) became the first female to referee boys' games in the U.S.A. These may have been small steps, but they showed that attitudes toward women in sports had changed.

It was all too much for the ruling powers of football, who perceived the growing popularity of the women's game as a threat to the domination of men. It was, after all, a man's game—or at least that was the position of the FA Council when they declared, in

Girls just want to have fun! And to win. ➤

Mob Ball

There are several different versions of this popular game, a forerunner of soccer. The very name "mob ball" conjures up an assortment of images of people running, kicking, jumping, flailing, floundering, scoring, and sweating. You can use your legs, feet, and fists, you can punch and head-butt, you can break down doors and climb over houses. It's the game of Ba' ("ball" in Scottish)—rough, tough, and very, very old. One species of Ba' is played in Kirkwall, a town on the Orkney Islands in Scotland. The two teams are the Uppies (from the north side of the town) and the Doonies (from the south side). Part rugby, part soccer, part bash, and part brawl, the game is usually played only on Christmas and on New Year's Day.

To win, the Doonies must dip the ba', a three-pound leather ball, into the harbor at Kirkwall, and the Uppies have to touch it against a wall at the south end of town. Other than that, there are no rules and no such thing as a foul. Players can climb over people's houses, kick people, and/or smash windows, eating and drinking as they go, and the game can last for hours. Concussions, crushed ribs, and broken legs are common injuries. And bruises, because onlookers tend to trip players and whack them with canes or umbrellas as they surge by.

Some people believe that mob ball originated about a thousand years ago when two groups of Vikings got to kicking around the head of an enemy, and it became a tradition. The game is pretty much unchanged except the head has been replaced by a leather ball.

December 1921: "Complaints having been made as to football being played by women, the Council feel impelled to express their strong opinion that the game of football is quite unsuitable for females and ought not to be encouraged . . . the Council request clubs belonging to the Association to refuse the use of their grounds for such matches."

At a stroke, the development of women's soccer was dramatically halted. Despite the rapid formation of the English Ladies Football Association (ELFA), the game was forced underground and spent almost half a century fighting bravely for recognition. But with no access to any but the most basic pitches and with no league structure, there was little in the way of organized women's football, and only the most dedicated teams played on a regular basis.

Mob Rules Soccer

This game of soccer is different from mob ball, although both games require mobs. It is played with a regular ball on a regular field, and on a much, much larger scale. Two teams of 128 players don numbers and contrasting colors and they hit the field for an invigorating, if somewhat crowded, soccer game. When one team scores, the other team must leave the field. The scoring team then splits into two new opposing teams, and play resumes with 64 players on each side. The process continues until 8 goals have been scored and one player remains on the field. That person is the victor, and wins a prize—usually an elaborate crown.

Pretinha and Roseli celebrate their win for the Washington Freedom at the inaugural WUSA match, 2001. Pretinha scored the first goal in WUSA history. ➤

A few years later, when the Great Depression hit, it not only brought economic turmoil, it paved the way for a backlash against the political and social advances women had made over the previous decades. Women's soccer went into a decline and did not recover until after World War II. Even then, the push for the women's game began outside of the traditional soccer hotbed of England. Italy, Scandinavia, and West Germany were early supporters, and West Germany hosted the first women's European Championships in 1957. England won the inaugural tournament, defeating the German squad 4–0 in the final.

The Communist countries of eastern Europe proved to be particularly active. Those governments valued team sports as a good social and physical outlet for men and women, and by the early 1960s, state-run sports clubs in Czechoslovakia and other countries were producing female soccer players of the highest caliber. At the same time, other populations around the world were starting to recognize the health benefits for children of physical activity, and youth soccer, a relatively inexpensive sport, was growing by leaps and bounds.

By the late 1960s women's soccer associations had formed in several countries, including Italy and France, which hosted an unofficial Women's World Cup in 1968. That same year, Pierre Geoffroy put

Slide-check WUSA style, offered up by Erica Iverson, number 14 (Philadelphia Charge), against Bai Jie (Washington Freedom). ▼

Women's soccer is the fastest growing team sport in the world. ➤

together his famous Féminin Reims women's team, which toured the world and played before sellout crowds. Within the year, even the stuffy old Football Association had to agree that women's soccer was not going to go away. They lifted their sixty-seven-year ban on women's football and, three years later, sanctioned the formation of the Women's Football Association. By then the women's game was recognized in most European countries and in parts of Asia and South America, and was played in thirty-five countries around the world.

The last stronghold of resistance was North America, where professional men's soccer dominated the national consciousness. But in 1977, Brown University in Rhode Island became the first American College to establish a varsity soccer program for women. Informal national women's collegiate championships were held in 1980, and two years later the National Collegiate Athletic Association held its first championships. With its foot in the door, women's soccer quickly took hold as the fastest growing sport in U.S. colleges, and by the end of the 1990s it had become one of the most popular participation sports for women in the U.S. and Canada, and around the world.

Title IX and After

In June 1972, the United States government enacted Title IX of the
Educational Amendments, stating that no one living in the U.S.A.
could be excluded from participating in any federally funded "educational program or activity"—including sports—on the basis of gender.
Thirty years later, the impact of Title IX is unmistakable. By 2003
there were more women athletes and more sports programs for
women than ever before.

Still, there's a lot of work to be done before women find equality
in the world of college sports. Females make up only 42 percent of
high school and varsity athletes, and the total number of females
playing college sports today is still lower than the number of males
who played back in 1972, the year Title IX became law.

Meanwhile, although women make up more than half the popu-
lation at college campuses, they receive far less than 50 percent of
the sports funding. At the Division I level in 2000, colleges spent
almost twice as much on recruiting and scholarships for boys than
they did for girls. Across the board, women make up 53 percent of
college students, but have only 41 percent of the opportunity to play
sports at a varsity level and 43 percent of scholarships.

At the same time, Title IX is under attack from conservative law-
makers who claim that the advances realized by the law have come at
the expense of men's programs. The facts don't support this line of
reasoning, but that doesn't stop the opponents. The fight for women's
rights on the sports fields of America is far from over.

◄ Norway's number one keeper, Bente Nordby, psychs up the crowd at the Olympic Games in Sydney, Australia, 2000.

CHAPTER 3

Women's Soccer and the Olympics

Atlanta, 1996: Lighting the Torch

The Olympic Games were the last bastion to fall in the world of women's soccer. When the 1996 games were scheduled to be played in Atlanta, Georgia, women's soccer wasn't even on the program. The organizers of the international sportsfest are traditionally slow to adapt to change, and seem to have dragged their heels particularly hard when it comes to adding sports for women. At the time of the Atlanta Games, only 36 percent of the athletes were women.

It took a tremendous individual effort to get women's soccer included in the XXVI Olympiad. In 1991 the Olympic organizers had cast a shadow over the hopes of women players around the world, announcing that it was "highly unlikely" their game would be represented in Atlanta in 1996. But female players did not concede defeat. In fact, they were just that much more determined to realize their Olympic dream. The drive was led by a determined woman named Marilyn Childress, the manager of a precision machine shop in Atlanta, who had started playing organized soccer when she was in her thirties. Childress carried her love of the game all the way to the Olympic organizing committee, gathering hundreds of supporters along the way. She even organized a test game in Atlanta to show the committee that the women's game was ready, willing, and able to participate in the greatest sports show on earth. Her hard work paid off. In 1993 the organizing committee met and agreed to make women's soccer a medal sport in the upcoming Olympic Games.

Women's soccer had won the day, but now it was under tremendous pressure to mount a successful tournament. There was not enough time to run proper qualifying games, so FIFA sent the top eight teams from the 1995 Women's World Cup. The only change was Brazil, which entered the Olympic tournament in place of England.>

Namely Soccer

The word "soccer" comes from a contraction of the word "association." The story goes that back in 1823, a group of English students at Rugby School got bored with kicking a ball down a field. A boy named William Webb Ellis, to the amazement of his friends and teammates, picked up the ball and ran to the other team's goal—and that's how rugby got started. The game caught on quickly, although it kept the name "football." Soon it rivaled regular old football in popularity, and people confused the "kickers" and the "runners." To clear things up, a group of forward thinkers got together in 1863 and formed the London Football Association, which was dedicated to advancing the cause of the "kickers." In time, traditional football came to be known as "association" football, and eventually "soccer" for short.

◄ Tiffany Milbrett of Team U.S.A. proves her mettle against Denmark at the Olympic Games in Atlanta, Georgia, 1996.

Team U.S.A. coach Tony
DiCicco celebrates Olympic
Gold with his winning team
at the Olympic Games,
Sanford Stadium, Atlanta,
Georgia, 1996. ▼

Pretinha leads her Team
Brazil to a strong showing at
the Women's World Cup,
Pasadena, 1999. ➤

The competition was close. Unlike in previous World Cup play, there were few blowouts. In the preliminary round robin, Denmark lost to powerhouse China 5–1 and Japan was soundly beaten 4–0 by Norway, but otherwise the games were close. It was clear the pool of talent in women's soccer was growing.

The semi-finals pitted the surprising Brazilians against China. After finishing ninth in the 1995 Women's World Cup, the Brazilian side had taken women's soccer by storm. Brazil played tough with its budding superstars Elane and Nene (key defenders), Pretinha and Katia (power strikers), Sissi (a free-kick specialist), and other players, and what it lacked in team discipline it made up for in individual skill. Not bad for a country with barely three hundred women playing organized soccer.

In their first game, Brazil tied the reigning world champion Norway, scoring the tying goal with two minutes left to play, and closed the round robin with a draw against Germany, a 1995 World Cup finalist. Meanwhile, China finished the preliminary round with two wins and a draw, the same record as team U.S.A. But China was seeded first, having scored 2 more goals than the Americans.

The game between Brazil and China was hard fought. The amazing Brazilians were leading 2–1 with barely seven minutes left

Sonia Denoncourt—
Woman with a Whistle

You may not recognize her name, but you're likely to remember Sonia Denoncourt as the woman with the whistle in some of the biggest soccer games of the last decade.

Her list of firsts is impressive. Not only was she the only Canadian, male or female, to be named to ref at the Sydney Olympics, she was also the first woman to oversee a professional First Division men's game and men's premier division season opener, and the first woman ever placed on the FIFA women's referees list.

Denoncourt continues to work hard on and off the pitch. A vegetarian who neither smokes nor drinks, she follows a rigorous training regimen and forgoes FIFA's fitness test for female referees in favor of the strenuous one for men.

Denoncourt is an in-demand referee on the world and professional circuits, and has come a long way since calling the shots at weekend soccer games in her hometown of Sherbrooke, Quebec. And in the process, she's taken the world of women's soccer a long way as well.

in regulation play when the Chinese coach decided to insert striker Wei Haiying into the lineup. Amazingly, she popped in 2 goals by the end of regulation time.

The other semi featured a powerhouse match-up as Norway faced the United States. Once again the hometown favorites, the American team was packed with stars like Mia Hamm, Michelle Akers, and Tiffeny Milbrett. But the Norwegians, fielding a squad almost identical to the one that had taken on the World Cup months earlier, took an early lead with forward Linda Medalen notching a goal at the eighteen-minute mark. The Americans held tight, tying the goal late in the game and eventually winning it in the tenth minute of extra time.

The final was played on August 1, before a full house at the 78,000-seat Sanford Stadium in Athens, Georgia. It was the largest crowd ever to watch a women's sporting event to that point, and these fans were only outnumbered by the ones who watched the Women's World Cup final three years later in Los Angeles. It was a game of contrasts, pitting the experienced veteran-loaded American team against the younger, up-and-coming Chinese team, which had already scored a tournament-leading 10 goals. They had met once before in the preliminary rounds, a battle of wills that ended in a 0–0 draw. As expected, the gold medal game was tightly contested. The U.S. took an early lead, only to see the Chinese draw even after thirty-two minutes. Just after an hour of play, the ever-reliable

Gro Espeth, number 5 (Norway), holds the ball away from a defending Team U.S.A. player at the Olympic Games in Sydney, Australia, 2000. ▼

Enjoying a little quality time on the field, Joy Fawcett hunkers down between her teammates Mia Hamm and Kristine Lilly to give the term "soccer mom" new meaning, at the Women's World Cup, Sweden, 1995. ➤

Tiffeny Milbrett knocked in what proved to be the game winner. The fans went wild, and the fate of women's soccer as an Olympic sport was sealed.

Sydney, 2000: The Flame Burns On

Four years later, there was no question about whether women's soccer deserved to be at the Olympics. The real question was: Would the American team make it to the XXVII Games in Sydney, Australia? Fresh from their 1999 World Cup victory, the American team encountered their toughest opponent yet—the U.S. Soccer Federation, governing body for the sport across the United States. The issues were pay and other perks, with Team U.S.A. players demanding equality with their male counterparts. As it stood, the women got between $2,000 and $3,500 per month for training, and an additional $250 for every game they played, but the men's team got $5,000 a month and a $2,000 bonus for every game.

For its part, the USSF maintained that unlike the men's team, the women's team lost money, and revenue streams for women's soccer were limited. For example, the U.S. men's team got about $2.4 million from FIFA for taking part in the 1998 World Cup, including $20,000 for each member just for making it to the Cup and a $35,000 playing bonus, even though Team U.S.A. finished dead last

Joy Fawcett—The Great Defender

Perhaps the greatest female defender of all time, Fawcett has been a fixture on the American National Team since the early 1990s. She starred for her country at the 1995 Women's World Cup, the 1996 Olympics, the 1999 Women's World Cup, and the 2000 Olympics, where she was one of only two players not to miss a single minute of play. With 24 goals to her credit by the end of 2000, Fawcett is the all-time top-scoring defender for the American team. She is shown here keeping the ball away from Zhao Lihong (China).

Steffi Jones—
The Defense Never Rests

One of the best female players ever to come
out of Germany, Jones is a defensive force in
midfield. At 5'11" she brings size, speed, and
skill to her position. She also has a wealth of
international experience, having played more
than seventy international games for her country
since 1993. That year Jones joined the German
National Team, and she also played on the bronze
medal-winning German team in the 2000 Olympic
Games and the German 1999 Women's World
Cup team. In 2002 she joined the WUSA's
Washington Freedom.

in the tournament. Meanwhile, members of the 1999 world champion women's team each got a $12,500 prize for coming first, along with a $2,500 bonus for making it to the big show.

The dispute between the USSF and U.S.A. players quickly got ugly, and by early 2000 the women went on strike. They refused to take part in an exhibition tournament in Australia that January, forcing the USSF to field a team made up mostly of college players. With a major embarrassment looming at the upcoming Olympics, the USSF finally gave in. They granted the women's team equal pay for equal work, and helped set the stage for another exciting medal round.

America came into the 2000 games favorite to win it all again. But the winds of change had been blowing in women's soccer. There was increasing parity between teams, with programs in countries like Germany and Brazil taking tremendous strides. Most of the teams that had played in Atlanta were back, although Australia had replaced Japan (Pacific) and Nigeria was representing Africa. The preliminary round robin yielded a number of surprises. The always tough China failed to qualify for the finals, despite drawing the U.S. 1–1. Meanwhile, Germany and Brazil finished 1–2 in tight group play that saw four of the six games decided by a single goal.

Germany faced Norway in the first semi-final. It was a close, well-defended game that presented few opportunities at either end. The upstart Germans actually carried the play, and came close to putting the game away at least twice. But a defensive error by Tina Wunderlich of Germany with barely ten minutes left to play cost her team a goal, and Norway moved on to the finals. Meanwhile, the Americans had their hands full with Brazil. The veteran Americans played a disciplined game, but had a hard time penetrating the Brazilian defensive zone. At the other end of the field, individual Brazilian players demonstrated their superior ball-control skills, and were only kept off the scoreboard thanks to some hard work by the U.S.A. defenders. It was a feisty contest, with the referee handing out eight cautions, and it ended in a hard-fought goal. After just over an hour of play, Mia Hamm pounced on a loose ball that had squeezed behind the Brazilian keeper, Andreia.

After Germany earned its first soccer medal by blanking Brazil 2–1 in the bronze medal game, Norway and the U.S.A. took the field. As always, the Americans were favored to win, but not by much. Norway was an established powerhouse and had beaten the U.S. three times already that year in tournament play. They also were the only team to have an overall winning record against the

Hege Riise—Midfield Virtuoso

One of the most technically sound players in the
world and captain of the Norwegian National
Team, Riise is a midfielder who excels at both
offense and defense. She has scored almost
60 goals in an international career that spans
a decade and 175 matches. She was part of
Norway's gold medal team at the 1995 World Cup,
2000 Sydney Olympics, and 1993 European
Championships. In 1995 she was awarded the
World Cup's Golden Ball and Silver Boot awards,
for being tournament MVP and second leading
scorer. She's gone on to become one of the top
players in the pro ranks.

The action is fast and furious as Pretinha, number 12 (Brazil), goes for the ball against Joy Fawcett, number 14 (U.S.A.), and Tiffeny Milbrett at the Olympic Games, Sydney, 2000. ▼

Pu Wei (China) finds a little open space, and that's all she needs to make the play. ➤

Americans, having won fourteen and drawn two out of twenty-nine meetings since the first World Cup. Early on, it looked as if the game might be a rout. Five minutes into it, Mia Hamm collected a pass and fought off a challenge from Norway's captain, Goeril Kringen. She closed in on goal, pulling the goalkeeper out of position, then flicked a short pass to Tiffeny Milbrett, who had a wide-open net. Suddenly it was 1–0. The Americans continued to press. They dominated play for most of the first half but gave up a late goal, as Gro Espeseth hammered home a rare Norwegian corner kick.

Team Norway settled down in the second half and played an attacking game, based on their superior speed and prowess on the long ball. Their hard work paid off when a Ragnhild Gulbrandsen header found the back of the net with barely ten minutes left to play. If not for some last-second heroics, that might have been it for the Americans. But as the referee prepared to blow the final whistle, Tiffeny Milbrett outjumped the defender Goeril Kringen to head in a Mia Hamm cross. The game was tied 2–2. It would go to extra time.

The cat-and-mouse game continued into the additional period, and twelve minutes in, Hege Riise played a long ball deep into the

Briana Scurry—In the Net

One of the top goaltenders in the world, Scurry proves that you don't have to be big to play big. At 5′8″ she is shorter than most soccer goalies, but she stands tall in the net. She's appeared in nearly 120 international games for Team U.S.A., and holds team goalkeeping records for appearances, wins, and shutouts.

An all-round player, Scurry spent time as both a forward and goalkeeper during her college career at the University of Massachusetts. She recorded her first international start in March 1994, earning a shutout in a victory over Portugal. Since then she's been in goal for virtually every major game her team has played, including wins at the 1996 Olympic Games and the 1999 World Cup.

Team U.S.A. end. The American defender, Joy Fawcett, played the ball with her head, but it deflected to the side and headed right toward Norwegian substitute Dagny Mellgren. She quickly trapped the ball, played it to her feet, and shot it past the hands of the American goalie, Siri Mullinix. American captain Julie Foudy immediately appealed to the referee for a hand-ball call. She argued that the ball had hit Mellgren in the shoulder on the way down. But the ref disagreed and the goal stood. Norway had won its first Olympic gold medal in women's soccer, and solidified its reputation as one of the premier nations in the sport.

Futsal, Anyone?

Futsal is FIFA's official version of arena soccer. In an area the size of a basketball court, with touchlines instead of walls, teams of five face off in a fast-paced, high-scoring competition. Unlike arena soccer, where the surrounding boards add a curious element not found in the full-sided game, futsal emulates the game as it's played on the field. It's the small game, with the big heart.

Bettina Wiegmann—
The Bronze Age

One of Germany's most experienced players, Wiegmann has played in almost 120 games for her country, and is third on its all-time scoring list with 36 international goals. Along with appearances at the 2000 Olympics in Sydney, where Germany took home the bronze, Wiegmann has also helped her country win three European Championships. Her 1996 tally against Japan will be remembered as the first goal by a woman in Olympic soccer history. She is shown here in the thick of a game between her team (Boston Breakers) and the Washington Freedom.

◄ Even a flagrant foul play by
Silke Rottenberg (Germany)
can't stop the powerhouse
Mia Hamm, number 9
(U.S.A.).

C H A P T E R

4

At the Top of
Their Game

Women's Soccer Turns Pro

The international success of women's soccer at both the World Cup and Olympic levels raised the question: What next? To many, a women's professional league seemed the obvious answer. By the mid-1990s there was already one pro league for women in the world, Japan's L-League, but female players began to dream of developing a higher-profile platform both to showcase their sport and to help develop and sustain talent.

In an era when professional sports were booming in the burgeoning American economy, the U.S.A. seemed like a natural

**All-Star Patience Avre,
number 18 (Nigeria), proves
how good she really is
against Suzana (Brazil) at
the Women's World Cup,
Pasadena, 1999.** ➤

setting for a new women's league. A group of players from the
American National Team began advocating for a league, and by 1998
plans were in place to begin an eight-team league. Team sponsors
were signed and most of the National Team agreed to play—and
then, at the last minute, the whole thing fell apart. The U.S. Soccer
Federation, perhaps concerned about the impact the league would
have on the existing men's professional teams, pulled their support.
It was a huge letdown for players and fans alike.

Still, there were options for America's top-ranked players. The
W-League had started up in 1996, offering a semiprofessional experience for national and top collegiate players. Originally called the
United States Interregional Women's League, the W-League allowed
a limited number of professionals to play alongside some of the most
skilled amateur players in the country. The tremendous growth of
women's soccer in the mid-1990s was reflected in the success of the
W-League, which expanded so quickly that by 1998 it had to split
into two divisions: the nineteen-team W-1 elite division and the
lower-tier W-2 division, with eighteen teams. Around the same time,
the Women's Premier Soccer League got under way. While not a professional league, the WPSL was a California-based organization that
provided female players with the highest level of amateur competition. The success of both leagues proved to organizers that women's
soccer could be a hit at the box office as well as on the playing field.
With the buzz generated by the 1999 World Cup and the stage set,

Rough play on the soccer field as Sara Whalen and Kristine Lilly (U.S.A.) struggle to get the ball from Team China players. ▼

Carla Overbeck of Team U.S.A. gains momentum by using her head. ➤

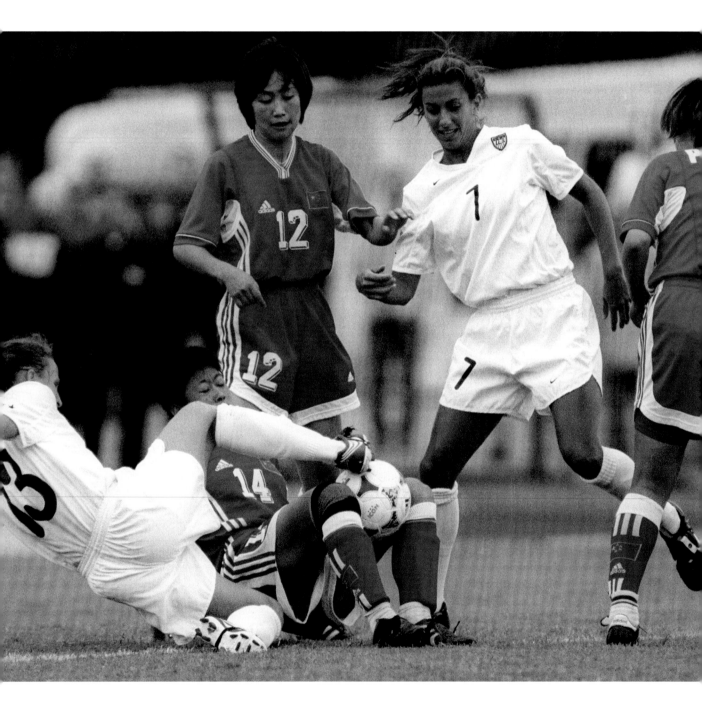

a group of marquee players, corporate sponsors, and media representatives got together early in 2000 to discuss the formation of the Women's United Soccer Association. The sponsors came through and committed $40 million to the league over the following five years. A few months later, in April, the WUSA was officially established, and the world of women's soccer suddenly had a premier professional league it could call its own.

The new league moved quickly to get ready for play. Eight cities were selected, as well as eight backup sites, and a number of high-profile players were signed up. At the same time, Turner Sports, the parent company of the television network TNT, agreed to broadcast eighty-eight games. Over the next few months, the league allocated all twenty members of Team U.S.A. to the new franchise, and also signed up a raft of stars from Brazil, Norway, China, and other teams. Finally, on November 2, 2002, after months of hard work in the boardrooms and backrooms, the WUSA announced its starting lineup of teams: Atlanta Beat, Bay Area CyberRays, Boston Breakers, New York Power, Carolina Courage, Philadelphia Charge, San Diego Spirit, and Washington Freedom. A month later the league held its first draft, with the Atlanta Beat making Chinese star Sun Wen—best player at the recent World Cup tournament—the first number one draft pick in WUSA history. That same day, the Atlanta Beat took

Maren Meinert— Team Player

**An international top goal-scorer and exceptional
playmaker, Meinert was a mainstay on Germany's
National Team for a decade, where she began
her playing career at age fifteen. She appeared
in almost eighty games and scored 25 goals,
more than almost anyone else in German
National Team history.**

    **Although she retired from international
play after helping her country with the 2001
European Cup, she continues to star for the
Boston Breakers of the WUSA. She scored the
first goal in Breakers history on May 21, 2001,
in a 1–0 win over Carolina.**

    **Meinert's league-leading assists usually go
to Dagny Mellgren, her teammate from Norway.**

Kara Lang, number 15 (Canada), takes on a young Mexican defender at an Under-19 game. ▼

Patience is a virtue—especially if it's Patience Avre, captain of the Nigerian National Team. ➤

part in the WUSA's first-ever trade, sending sixth-round pick to the San Diego Spirit for Kerry Gragg.

Finally, after more than three years of waiting for a professional league, players and fans got their wish. On April 14, 2001, in RFK Stadium in Washington, D.C., the San Jose CyberRays, featuring Brandi Chastain, kicked off against Mia Hamm and the home team Freedom in front of more than 34,000 fans. It was a close game, and it seemed destined to finish in a 0–0 draw. At the seventy-minute mark, Brazil's gifted scorer Pretinha was awarded a penalty shot. She wasted no time in scoring the first goal in WUSA history, a marker that would stand as the game winner.

The rest of the season continued smoothly. Playing mostly in college soccer stadiums, teams played twenty-one regular season games, with the top four teams making the playoffs and vying for the Founder's Cup. By the time the elimination round was finished, two teams were left in competition. It was the CyberRays versus the Atlanta Beat fighting it out for league bragging rights in front of 21,000 screaming fans at the Foxboro Stadium in Foxboro, Massachusetts.

The fans were treated to an action-packed game that went all the way to penalty kicks. The CyberRays got off to an early start—six minutes into the game, a free kick in the offensive zone found its way

Tiffeny Milbrett— Striker Extraordinaire

Milbrett may be the best female striker playing in the game today. She's the complete package— tremendous strength and speed on the ball, with a creative flair and an intuitive understanding of the game.

With more than 90 goals in just over 180 international games, Milbrett is currently third on the U.S. team's all-time scoring list, behind Mia Hamm and Michelle Akers. Her offensive prowess is also evident in the pros, and she's reigning points leader in WUSA history.

Milbrett started her soccer career at the University of Portland, where outstanding play earned her a spot on the U.S. Soccer College Team of the Decade in the 1990s. She made her first appearance on the National Team in 1992 against Norway, and by 1996 had entrenched herself as starting striker. She was there in 1996 when the U.S. won gold at the Olympics, scoring the medal-winning goal in the final game, and she led all-American scorers in the 1999 World Cup.

An outstanding athlete, Milbrett still has lots more soccer to play.

to Brandi Chastain. She headed it in for a 1–0 lead. But the Beat were equal to the task, putting on a passing clinic in the San Jose end. The play ended with Nancy Augustyniak dishing off a nice little pace to Kylie Bivens, standing alone in the penalty area. She hammered a shot past CyberRays keeper LaKeysia Beene and the score was tied.

The Beat kept coming, and three minutes later pulled ahead on a play started by goalkeeper Briana Scurry. She punted the ball downfield to Cindy Parlow, who headed forward, setting up Charmaine Hooper, who pulled behind the CyberRays defense. A quick chip later and the Beat were up by a goal. But the CyberRays did not give up. After being robbed twice by Scurry at the thirty-minute mark, they tied it up on a Julie Murray breakaway.

The wild and wooly first half was followed by a more conservative second, with both teams trying not to make a fatal mistake. It was late in the half when Sun Wen of Atlanta tapped a header from close in between the legs of defender Gina Oceguera. With less than seven minutes left, the game looked all but finished. But once again the Beat refused to quit, and within two minutes Tisha Venturini took a pass from the Brazilian Katia, and found herself behind the CyberRays defense alone on the goal. Just that quickly, the game was tied again. >

Carla Overbeck, number 4 (U.S.A.), catches a free ride on a Brazilian player. ➤

Seeing Double

Talk about double trouble! Julie and Nancy Augustyniak, twin sisters from Georgia, are a force to be reckoned with in the backfield. After stellar college careers, where they co-captained Clemson and earned numerous All-Star berths, the twins were drafted by the Atlanta Beat of the WUSA from their W-League team, the Atlanta Classics. In April 2002 they played against the Washington Freedom's Little twins, Jacqui and Skylar, marking the first time two sets of twins had faced each other in a major North American professional sporting event (Atlanta won, 1–0).

Never has there been such a match-up in any major professional sports league in North America—MLB, NFL or AFL, NBA or ABA, NHL, WNBA, MLS, or WUSA.

The WUSA boasts four sets of identical twins playing in the Division I women's professional soccer league. In addition to the Augustyniak and Little twins, the Fair sisters (Lorrie of the Philadelphia Charge and Ronnie of the New York Power) and the Tietjen twins (Jennifer of the Philadelphia Charge and Margaret of the San Diego Spirit) compete in the WUSA.

Sun Wen—Gold Rush

**The greatest midfielder in the history of
Chinese women's soccer and the first-ever pick
of the WUSA, Wen won both the Golden Ball
and Golden Boot awards, for top player and top
scorer respectively, at the 1999 World Cup.
That year she was also co-named FIFA's Female
Player of the Century.**

Follow the bouncing ball as
Natalia Barbachina, number
10 for Team Russia, tries to
outjump Joy Fawcett (U.S.A.)
at the Nike U.S. Women's
Cup, New York, 2002. ➤

The game went into overtime, but there was little room to maneuver as both teams went into a defensive shell. So it was off to penalty kicks. CyberRays keeper Beene put Atlanta in the hole from the start, making a terrific save off a Sun Wen shot. The fate of the game was sealed two rounds later, as Charmaine Hooper booted her kick wide. San Jose connected on their next two kicks and put the fame out of reach. It was a great ending to the first Founder's Cup championship, and an even better beginning to what players and fans hope will be a long sporting tradition.

Despite the immediate success of the playoffs and the league, there were repercussions throughout the world of women's soccer. Particularly affected were the Women's Premier Soccer League and

Cheryl Salisbury—Playing the Field

It's hard enough to become a world-class player at one position, but Cheryl Salisbury of Australia has managed to do it at three.

Born in 1974 and originally from Newcastle, Australia, Salisbury started her career in the midfield. She first represented her country in 1994 and went on to become Australia's all-time leading scorer in international play, with 25 goals.

But in 1999 she decided to make a switch. She moved back to defense, and became a veteran force on the backfield. By 2003 she was captain of the Matildas, but still found enough time to hone her skills in the WUSA, where she plays midfield for the New York Power.

The road to the WUSA was paved with a stint in the W-League, where Salisbury starred—as a forward. She scored 2 goals and added 2 assists for the Memphis Mercury in 2002, and added 3 goals in two games in the playoffs, before being called up to the Bigs.

the W-League. In the first two years of pro play, the WPSL lost more than seventy players to the WUSA, with one team, the California Storm of Sacramento, yielding fifteen players to the big league in 1991 alone. Meanwhile, the W-League adapted to the changes and repositioned itself as a development league for the WUSA, helping to create an environment where the best amateur players could build their skills on the road to a professional career.

Still, the impact of the WUSA was huge. Now female players around the world had a dream to work toward—a dream that came with substantial financial rewards. Today's WUSA players make between $24,000 and $85,000 per season, with the promise of revenue sharing as the league grows, and many of the stars have signed lucrative endorsement deals with shoe and equipment companies. It also gives the women a chance to play with the best soccer players on earth, everyone from American stars like Brandi Chastain, Mia Hamm, Tiffeny Milbrett, and Briana Scurry, to Norway's Gro Espeseth, Bente Nordby, and Hege Riise, to the Brazilians Pretinha and Roseli. Meanwhile, the ideal of developing elite professional leagues for women seems to be catching on. The WUSA has the best women's league in the world but it is not the only one. Other leagues throughout Europe and Asia were established before 2001 and new professional women's leagues will become more and more popular as time goes on. Whether they approach the success, popularity, and competitive level of the WUSA is another question, but nations like England, Sweden, Norway, Germany, Japan, China, and Australia

Svetlana Sedakova takes a kick for Team Russia at the Nike U.S. Women's Cup, New York, 2002. But it wasn't good enough— the U.S. women's team dominated the game and brought in a 5–1 victory. ➤

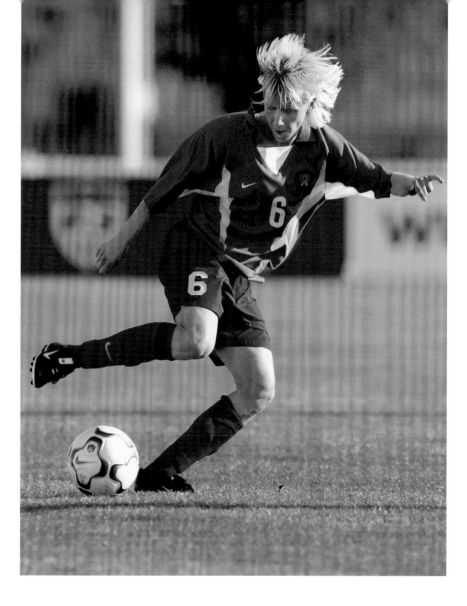

Ice and Fire

Iceland's prospects are heating up with young players like Margret Olafsdottir and Rakel Karvelsson waiting in the wings. Both members of Iceland's National Team, they found themselves teammates again playing for the Chicago Charge of the WUSA.

Brandi Chastain, number 6
of the San Jose CyberRays,
plays keep-away with Mia
Hamm of the Washington
Freedom, in the inaugural
WUSA match at RFK Stadium
in Washington, D.C., 2001. ➤

will be part of the leagues of the future. And women's club teams have emerged in places like Brazil, Mexico, and Africa, gaining respect while continuing to grow at remarkable speed.

Since 1993, when the Football Association officially endorsed women's soccer in Britain, the sport has made tremendous strides. Along with a new development program for women's soccer, with an eye to getting an English side in the 2007 World Cup, the FA has also established a premier league and a Women's FA cup—both moves designed to encourage excellence on the field. As well, England got its first professional team in 1999. Fulham, located in the London area, compiled an astonishing 38–0 record over two seasons, outscoring their opponents 324–9. But in the end, success may have contributed to the team's downfall. With a lack of adequate competition, and most games ending in blowouts, Fulham lost money and finally downgraded to semiprofessional status in 2002. Still, the FA remains committed to women's professional soccer in Britain, and hopes to have a league in place in the very near future.

Marinette Pichon—The French Connection

Pichon has been a mainstay with the French National Team since 1996, and she has developed into one of the top offensive players in the WUSA. In 2002 she was named the league's MVP and Offensive Player of the Year, as well as earning first team All-Star honors. Her hard work and undisputed talent helped France earn its first World Cup berth, in 2003.

◄ Shannon MacMillian (U.S.A.)
proves that there's only one
way to fly, in a game against
Brazil at the Olympic Games,
Sydney, Australia, 2000.
Team U.S.A. came back from
Down Under with silver.

5

It's a
Small World

The 2003 World Cup and Beyond

The months leading up to the 2003 World Cup were yet another showcase for the talents of the greatest female soccer players on the planet. This fourth installment of FIFA's championship was scheduled to be held in the U.S.A. and to feature teams from sixteen countries. Excitement about the event and the elite level of play were a tribute to how much women's soccer had grown in just over a decade. Countries around the world are fielding competitive teams and proving that the fastest-growing sport in the world is here to stay.

Kara Lang, Team Canada
U-19, in fine form and pitch-
perfect action. She played
all five games at the 2002
Gold Cup. ➤

AUSTRALIA

Australia's national women's soccer team has slowly developed into a steady force. Officially called the Quantas Matildas, the team first entered international play in October 1979, when they held traditional rival New Zealand to a 2–2 draw. Since 1995 they have been a fixture at the World Cup, finishing twelfth out of twelve teams that year but moving up to finish eleventh out of sixteen teams in 1999. The trend continued at the 2000 Olympics, where the Matildas came in seventh and gave many of the top teams a run for their money. The year and a half leading up to the 2003 World Cup saw the Australians post victories against top-ranked teams such as China, Japan, Mexico, and Russia.

BRAZIL

The Brazilian side continues to improve, despite the relatively low number of players in that country. Like other South American soccer players, the Brazilians are highly skilled and display tremendous ball control. After coming out of nowhere to finish third in the 1999 World Cup, the Brazilians followed with a fourth-place finish at the 2000 Olympics. Led by veteran stars like Pretinha, widely recognized as one of the most dangerous strikers in the world, Katia, who tied fourth in scoring at the Sydney Olympics, and Sissi, a free-kick specialist, the Brazilians are also looking for support from their younger players. At the Under-19 World Cup in 2002, at which the up-and-coming player Marta scored a spectacular hat-trick, the Brazilian team tied with Canada for the most goals in the

Liu Ailing—Front and Center

One of the strongest players ever to come from China, Ailing retired from active competition in 2002. She rarely missed a game in her long and distinguished international career, which started in 1987. With more than 80 goals to her credit, and appearances at three World Cups and two Olympics, Ailing played a key role in putting the Chinese women's soccer team on the map.

Kristine Lilly, number 13 of the WUSA's Boston Breakers, brushes off the defense of Emmy Barr (number 2) and Kacy Beitel (number 21) of the Washington Freedom. ▼

Sissi of Team Brazil shows her colors, but she is also a member of the WUSA. In 2002 she was named to the All-WUSA first team, and was also named WUSA Humanitarian of the Year. ➤

tournament and finished fourth overall, after losing to Germany in a shootout.

CANADA

Canada is one of the up-and-comers on the international scene. In the 2002 championship of the Confederation of North, Central American and Caribbean Association Football, CONCACAF for short, the Canadians outscored their opponents 25–1 going into the final. Even though they lost the final to Team U.S.A. in a 2–1 thriller, the team earned a berth in the 2003 World Cup. Two of the players, Charmaine Hooper and Christine Sinclair, tied with America's Tiffeny Milbrett for top scorer in the tournament.

Over the past few years, the National Team has posted wins over the U.S.A., China, Denmark, France, and Australia. And while the senior players are making inroads, the junior team also shows tremendous potential. At the 2002 Under-19 Women's World Cup, held in Canada, the home team put on a dazzling performance. Posting strong wins against Denmark, Japan, and Nigeria, Team Canada met England in the quarter-finals. Enter teenage phenom Christine Sinclair, eventual tournament MVP and winner of both the Golden Boot and the Golden Ball, who notched an unbelievable 5 goals en route to a 6–2 Canadian win. After beating Brazil on penalty kicks, the young Canadian met the U.S.A. in the final.

Julie Foudy—All-American Leader

A born leader, Foudy is captain of both the U.S. National Team and the San Diego Spirit of the WUSA.

Originally from Mission Viejo, California, Foudy was a four-time All-American at Stanford University and joined Tiffeny Milbrett on the U.S. Soccer College Team of the Decade. She also served as 2003 president of the Women's Sports Foundation.

Foudy was accepted into Stanford's med school, but she decided instead to concentrate on soccer, and the sport is richer for it. She began her National Team career in 1988 at age seventeen, and three years later started at midfield on the inaugural World Cup-winning team of the U.S.A. Now, with more than 100 points and 200 caps in international play, Foudy is one of the most celebrated players in American history. She is a fifteen-year veteran of the U.S. Women's National Team, with over 200 appearances to date.

It may look like the chicken
dance, but both Kristine Lilly,
number 13 (U.S.A.), and
Steffi Jones, number 4
(Germany), clean their
spikes and train their eyes
on the ball at the 100th
anniversary of the German
Soccer Federation (DFB),
Germany, 2000. ➤

Almost 50,000 fans watched the home team go down to defeat in the 109-minute contest, but not before the national program had earned the respect of the soccer world.

CHINA

Always a top competitor, the Chinese National Team is going through a period of transition as older players step aside and younger players strive to prove themselves. China finished out of the medals in the inaugural World Cup in 1991, but four years later, a drastically improved team made it all the way to the final four, just missing out on the medals with a loss to the U.S.A. That set the scene for the following year at the Atlanta Olympics, where the two teams met again in the final. China won the silver medal, and showed the world that they were a force to be reckoned with. In 1999 the two teams faced off once more in the World Cup final. It was a thrilling game, which ended in extra time at a 0–0 draw. The U.S. again triumphed in shootout, but China went home with another trip to the medal podium. Concerns about the outbreak of the virus SARS, which caused FIFA to move the 2003 World Cup out of China and to the U.S.A., was a blow to the Chinese team, but the players have dug deep and vowed to stay strong in the face of adversity.

ENGLAND

Since the FA officially threw its support behind women's soccer in 1993, the sport has taken off in merry old England. By 2003 more than five thousand females were playing organized soccer in

Charmaine Hooper — Global Fast Forward

Hooper is simply the best female player Canada has ever produced. She has appeared in almost 100 international matches, and her 56 goals stood as a national record to the end of 2003.

Hooper had an outstanding college career at **North Carolina State**, where she earned two NSCAA All-American nods and three All-ACC First-Team selections, and led her team to an ACC championship in 1988.

After six years in the W-League, where she helped the **Chicago** win the 2000 title, she moved to the WUSA and has been a fixture there ever since. Recognized as one of the top offensive players in the professional game, she was named to the league's Global First Team in 2002.

Hooper is also Canada's most experienced international player. She represented her country in the 1995 and 1999 Women's World Cups, and helped lead Canada into the 2003 tournament, scoring 7 goals in the prestigious 2002 Gold Cup. She is a two-time World All-Star.

It's two on one as Zhang Ouying, number 7 (China), tries to outrun Carla Overbeck, number 4 (U.S.A.), and a teammate. ▼

Zhao Lihong (China) shows her stuff at a WUSA match. She joined the Chinese National Team in 1992 and went on to serve as midfielder for the Philadelphia Charge. ➤

England, ten times the number playing when the FA ban was lifted, and thousands of other women enjoy the sport throughout the United Kingdom.

While it was slow to embrace the game, England's soccer establishment has thrown itself wholeheartedly behind the growth and development of the women's sport. The team has an ambitious goal—to win the World Cup in 2007. In support of that objective, they've set up coaching centers and club programs for girls around the country, elite soccer academies with professional coaches and facilities, an international player development center, and a series of elite leagues culminating in the Women's Premier Division, with teams vying for their own FA Cup. The hard work is paying off as the National Team continues to gain respect around the world. And while they didn't earn a trip to the 2003 World Cup, losing to France in the tough European Football Association qualifying round, they are quickly making a name for themselves on the international scene.

Germany

Thanks to a comprehensive development program that culminates in the elite women's Bundesliga, Germany has moved into a position of dominance among European women's teams. The Germans play an exceptional technical game, which emphasizes teamwork and an

Even Pellerud—The Winning Edge

Canada wanted to get that winning edge when they went looking for a new coach to head the national women's program. And they may just have found it in Even Pellerud.

Former head coach of the women's program in Norway during the early 1990s, Pellerud helped his country secure the respect of the international soccer community. His team captured the gold at the 1995 World Cup, to go along with second-place silver at the 1991 world tournament and a bronze medal in 1996 at the Sydney Olympics, and European Cup triumphs.

Pellerud, who was named Canada's head coach in the fall of 1999, seemed to light a fire under his team from the start. Shortly after he took over, the rising Canadian team beat Finland 2–1 in Portugal's prestigious Algarve Cup and continued to improve, eventually beating Mexico in a November 2002 Gold Cup semi-final game, to clinch a place at the 2003 Women's World Cup.

German players are making their mark, as Hege Riise of Norway (left) finds out from Germany's Maren Meinert at the Women's World Cup, Sweden, 1995. ▼

A feisty midfielder with a scoring flair, Monica Gerardo has been a member of the Mexican National Team since 1998. After apprenticing in the U.S. Under-20 National Team system for a few years, Gerardo, who is eligible to play in both countries, played a key role in helping Mexico qualify for its first Women's World Cup in 1999. In her first three years of WUSA play, Gerardo scored 19 goals in just over forty games. ➤

organized attack, and they are capable of beating almost anyone. The team has fared well in recent years, winning the European Championship in 1995, 1997, and 2001, an Olympic bronze medal at the 2000 games in Sydney, Australia, and second place in the 1995 Women's World Cup. They capped their drive to the 2003 World Cup by finishing number one in the European qualifiers, thanks to a strong performance by players like Martina Müller, Bettina Wiegmann, and of course striker Birgit Prinz. The WUSA star has been a fixture on the German team since making her international debut in 1995. She's scored an incredible 39 goals in ninety-one international games for her country, and came in fourth for the 2001 World Player of the Year, behind Mia Hamm, Sun Wen, and Tiffeny Milbrett.

NORWAY

After the U.S.A., Norway may just have the strongest women's soccer program in the world. They've never been out of the top four in World Cup finishers, taking the gold in 1995 and silver in 1991, and having asserted their soccer supremacy in 2000 by defeating Team U.S.A. for an Olympic gold medal. The only team to boast an all-time winning record over the Americans, Norway has a mix of young players and proven veterans that should help ensure success for years to come.

U.S.A.

Team U.S.A. remains the dominant force in world women's soccer. An early favorite going into the 2003 World Cup, the team featured a balance of veteran experience and youthful ambition. It was full circle for veterans Brandi Chastain, Joy Fawcett, Julie Foudy, Mia Hamm, and Kristine Lilly, whose international career had started twelve years earlier at the inaugural World Cup in China. Meanwhile, the younger players are keeping the tradition of American soccer supremacy alive. Winners of the first-ever FIFA Under-19 Women's World Championship in 2002, this core of play-ers will join with the likes of midfielder Aly Wagner, defender Cat Reddick, and striker Shannon MacMillan, who led the American National Team in 2002 with 17 goals.

Although international competition is much tighter than ever before, the Americans still showed they were the ones to beat. Coming out on top at the 2002 Four Nations Tournament in China, the Algarve Cup in Portugal, and the Nike U.S. Women's Cup,

Sharolta Nonen—Back Beat

One of the rising stars of Canadian soccer, Nonen made her first international appearance in a 1999 loss to Brazil. Since then, she's played in more than forty games for her country. A three-time NSCAA All-Star at her college in Nebraska, this former Big 10 Player of the Year helped her country make a strong showing at the 2002 Gold Cup. A second-place finish in that tournament ensured this defender and her teammates a place in the 2003 World Cup.

where the team went undefeated for the ninth straight year, the Americans finished the year with only two losses and headed into the World Cup looking to defend their title of soccer supremacy.

A Look Ahead

Women's soccer has come a long way in a short time. Barely thirty years ago, few women were even playing the game. Within a decade, we saw the rise of recreational play, a dramatic increase in levels of play, and—finally—recognition of women's soccer on the world stage. And along the way, the game has developed to become the fastest-growing participation sport in the world.

So what does the future hold? More and more women will be playing the game at a higher level, developing their own skills and the capacity of their National Teams to compete at the international level. Meanwhile, women have already made inroads in the professional ranks. Not only is the number of professional leagues growing around the world, but female coaches and refs are finding their place in the man's game. Who knows? Maybe female strikers, sweepers, and keepers will be next.

The last three decades have been so much fun to watch, with so much drama and success, it's a pleasure to look ahead and imagine what the next three decades will bring. One thing's for certain: the passionate game that we call women's soccer is only going to get better and better. For many of us around the world, it's not just a game—it's way of life.

Jessica Ballweg, number 3 (U.S.A.), and Katie Thorlakson (Canada) keep their eyes on the ball at a FIFA U-19 world championship. Photo by Daniel Motz ➤

ACKNOWLEDGMENTS

Thanks to my husband and kids, and to all the wonderful people at Greystone Books. —Barbara Stewart

Thanks to my dad for introducing me to and teaching me the amazing game of soccer. —Helen Stoumbos

My small piece of this book is for Eric and Josh, always the pleasure of my life. My boys gave me the desire to show the world how I see it and, in turn, a career in photography. I am present in the soccer world because of the encouragement of Brett, my partner in life and the one that I love. —Pam Whitesell

This book is for my father, who taught me photography, believed in everything I did, and never witnessed the accomplishments. And for my wife Pam, because none of this would have been possible without her. —J. Brett Whitesell